The Usborne

Big Book
to
Color

Get coloring!

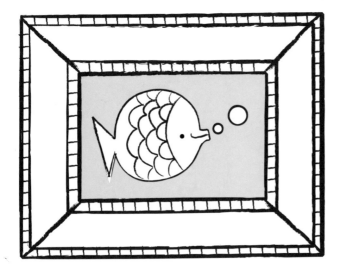
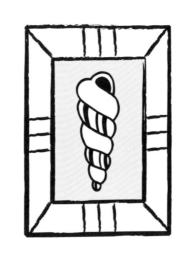
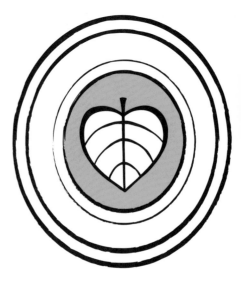

Pictures drawn by
Josephine Thompson,
Vicky Arrowsmith, Caroline Day
and Sam McPhilips

Words written by Anna Milbourne

First published in 2011 by Usborne Publishing Ltd., 83-85 Saffron Hill, London, EC1N 8RT, England www.usborne.com Copyright © 2011 Usborne Publishing Ltd. The name Usborne and the devices ♀⊕ are Trade Marks of Usborne Publishing Ltd. All rights reserved. No part of this publication may be reproduced, stored in a retrieval system, or transmitted in any form or by any means, electronic, mechanical, photocopy, recording or otherwise, without prior permission of the publisher. AE. American editor: Carrie Armstrong. First published in America in 2011. Printed in Dongguan, Guangdong, China.

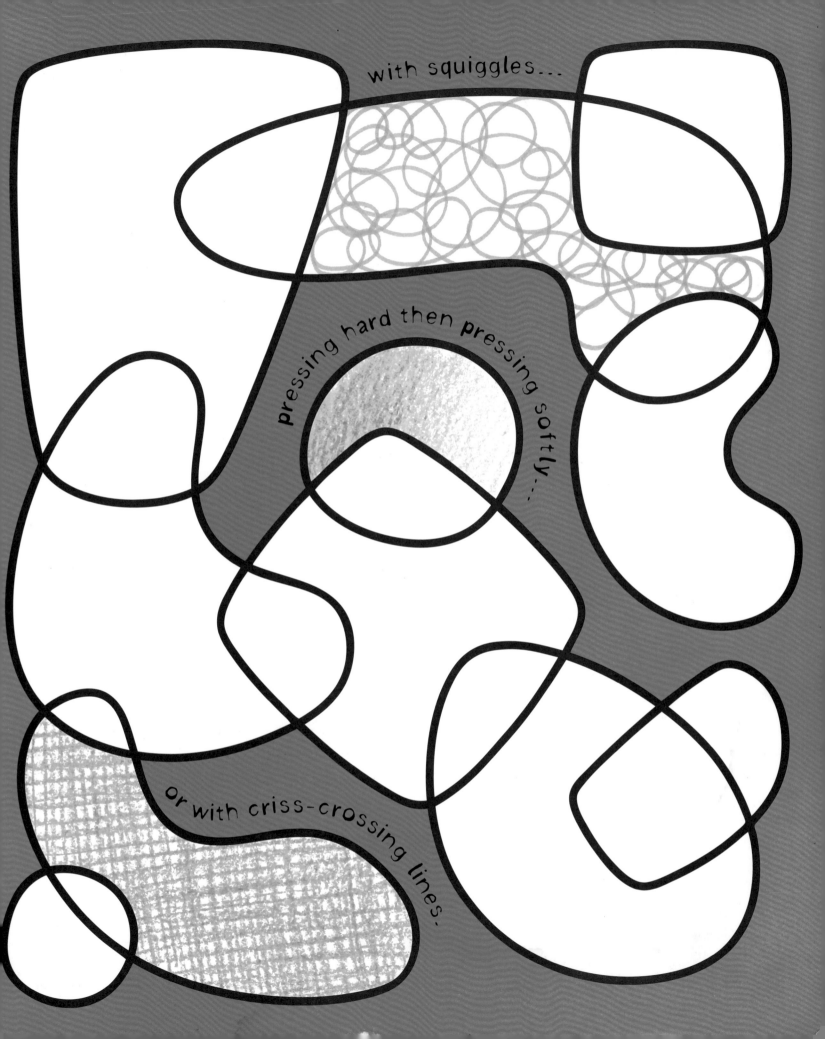

Make sure these bugs are nice and stylish.
They're going to a fancy Bug Ball...

This butterfly is the loveliest of them all!

Catch me if you can!

Follow the trails with a crayon to catch up with these snails.

9

This poodle loves her curly-wurly fur.

WOOF! WOOF!

This wiener dog might like more patches.

TWIT-TWOOO!

18

If you fill me with **pale** colors I can be seen in the dark.

If you fill me with dark colors I can hide at night.

19

Hello, my name is Lara.

I'm Natasha.

I'm Rosa.

20

Can you think of more names for these Russian dolls?

21

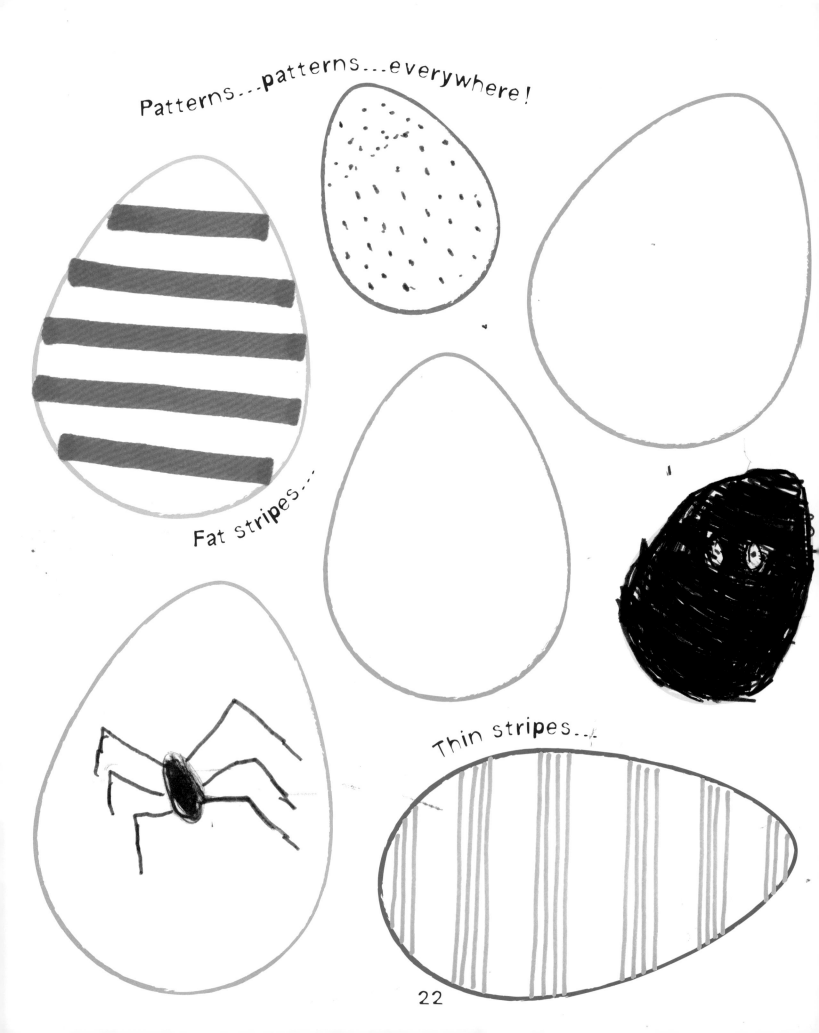

Patterns...patterns...everywhere!

Fat stripes...

Thin stripes...

22

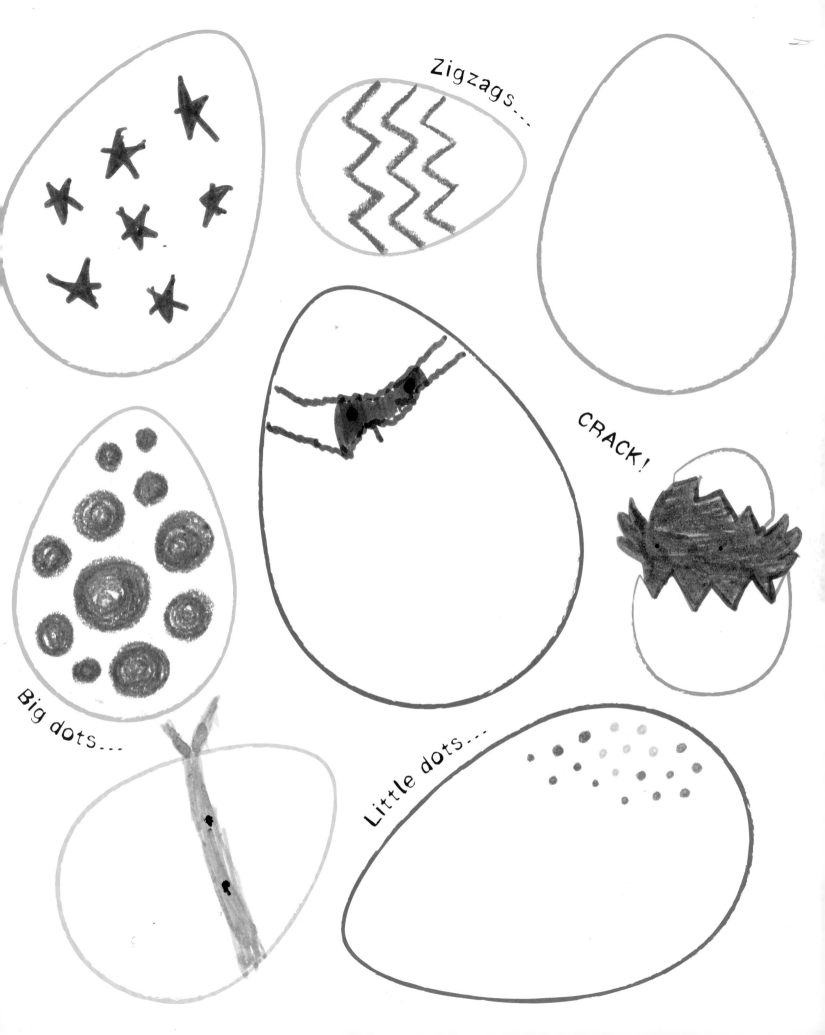

Zigzags...

CRACK!

Big dots...

Little dots...

These zebras need some stripes.

Do my stripes have to be black?

24

Honk!
Honk!

29

Some fish are as bright as bright can be...

Blub!

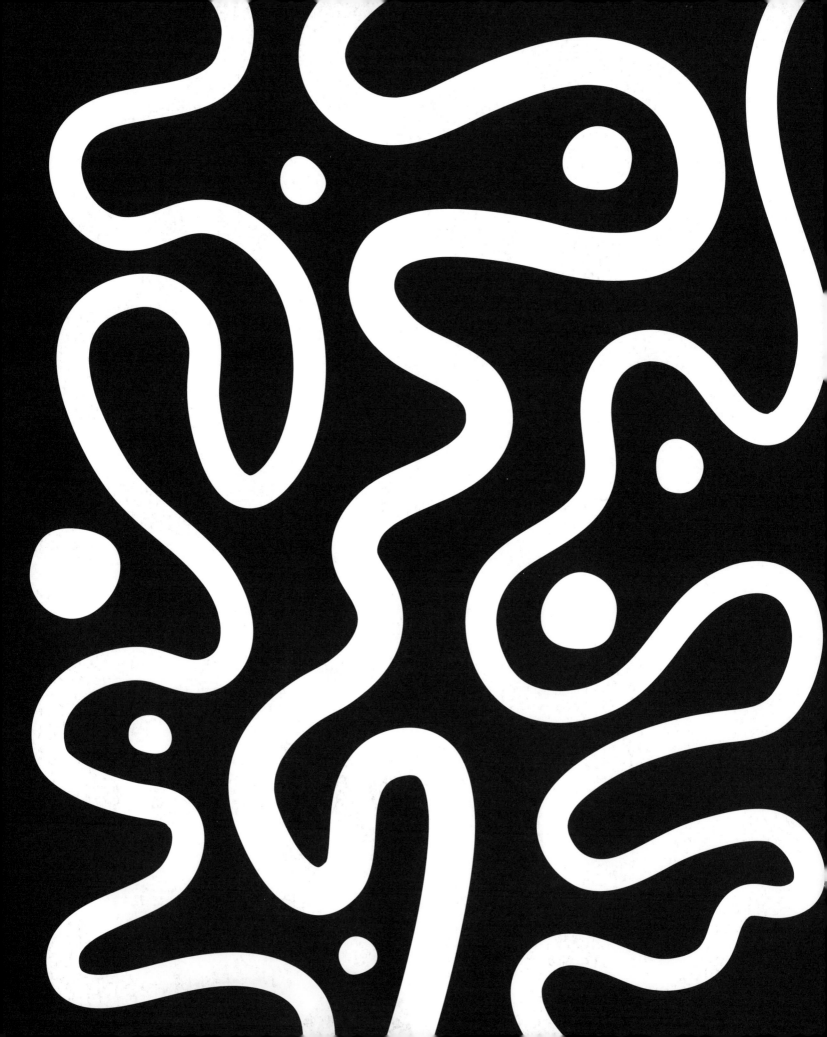

This gecko likes to show off.

Make him very colorful.

This gecko is shy.

If you color him green, he can hide.

36

Brrrr...wrap up warm!

Fill this scarf with the coziest colors you can find.

You could fill the spaces...

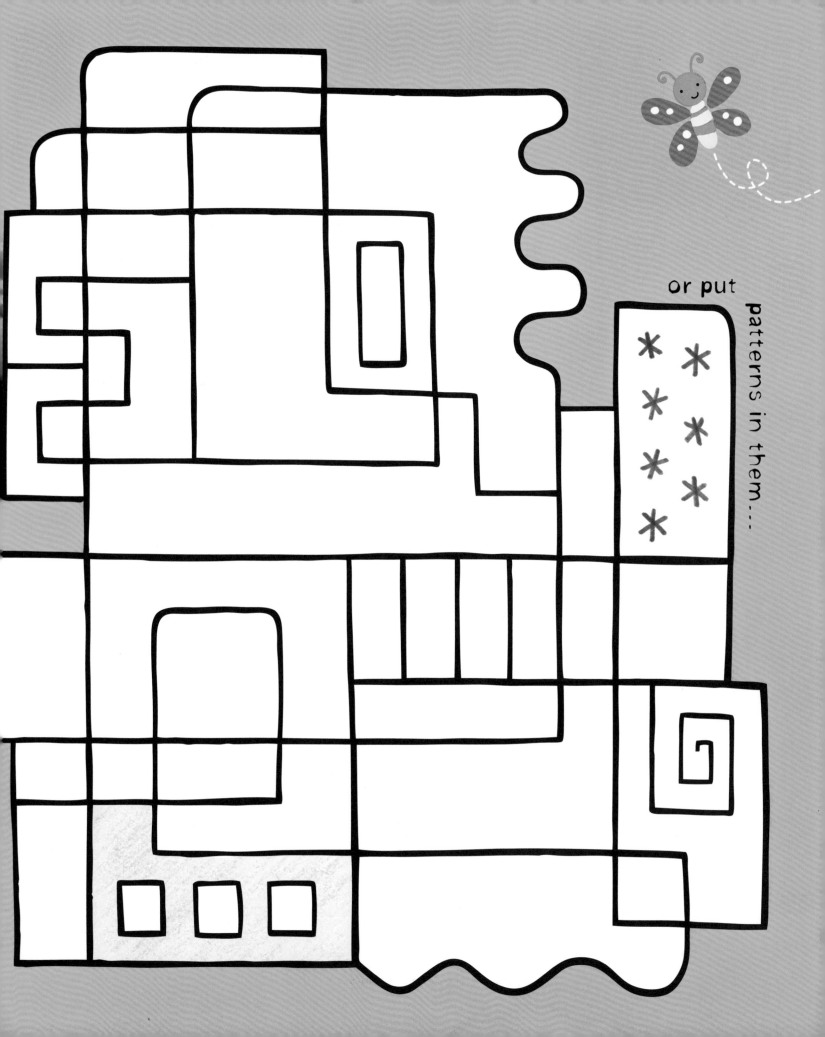

or put patterns in them...

43

44

Bob...bob...bob...

Bob...bob...bob...bob...

50

53

Watch out for the crocodiles' teeth...

SNAP!

SNAP!

SNAP!

55

You could do squiggly lines to fill this tree with bushy leaves.

Can you think of some more monster names?

62

Drizzle...drizzle...drizzle...

Isn't it nice and rainy?

These hungry hens and chicks
would like more little seeds to eat.

How many different colors can you use to fill these circles?

68

Flitter---flutter---

Buzz!

Buzz!

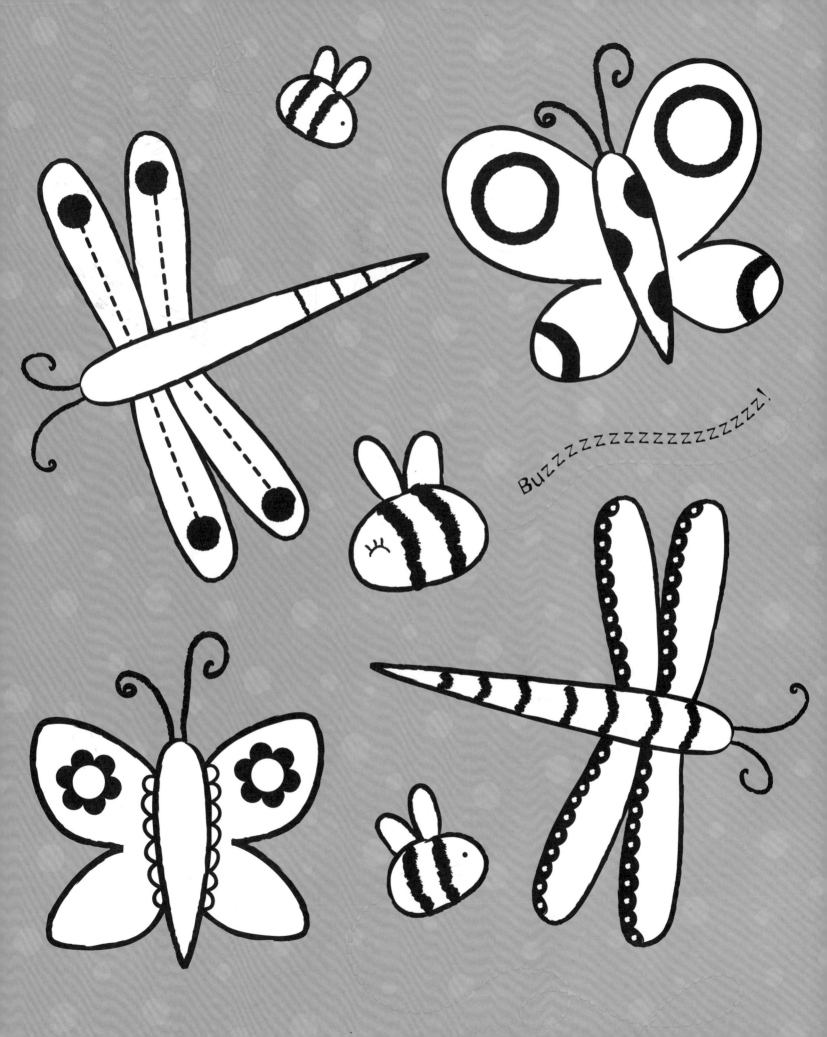

Buzzzzzzzzzzzzzzzz!

zonk-zonk.

Hello down there!

73

I love blue.

Does your favorite color look good on me?

Zooooom!

Whooooosh!

Fill this shape with squiggly cotton candy.

Go around and around to make a swirly lollipop.

80

What's your favorite flavor?

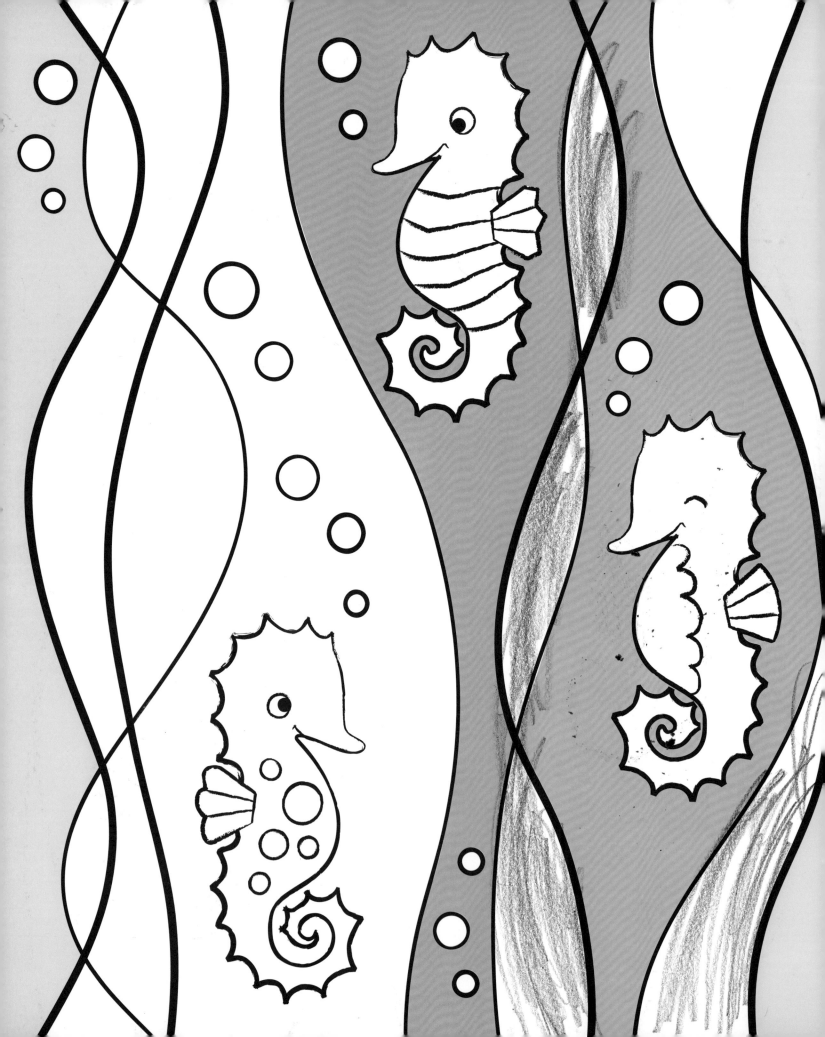

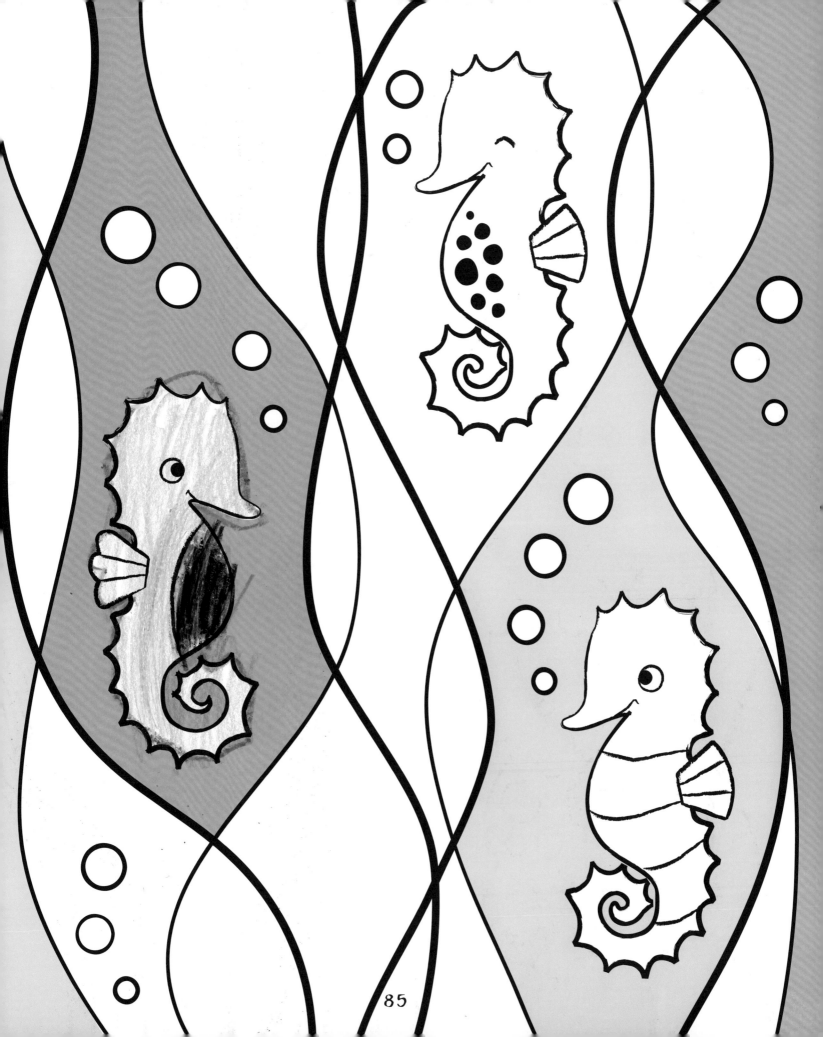

Let's go fly a kite...

Up...up...and away!

89

If you color these shapes in cool blues and purples they will look like ice-cold snowflakes.

If you color them in warm yellows, oranges and reds, they will look like fiery stars.

93

These flags look great with lots of patterns.

Can you make each one different from the rest?